D1165731

TWO HEARTS TALKING

by

Harald H. Prommel

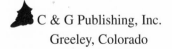

C & G Publishing, Inc.
Greeley, Colorado

TWO HEARTS TALKING

Copyright © 2000
by Harald H. Prommel

Library of Congress Catalog Card Number: 00-130390
ISBN 0-9626335-9-3
Printed in the United States of America

Illustrated by Kent Jackson
Graphic Design by Gregory Effinger, for CIGAR Graphics
Literary agent: Donna Jackson

Published by C & G Publishing, Inc.
PO Box 5199
Greeley, Colorado 80634-0103
For orders and information: 1-800-925-3172
Online at: www.cgpub.com

DEDICATION

This book is dedicated to the women of my family

. . .my mother, who made sure I had a heart to begin with.

. . .Betty, my wife, whose heart has talked with mine for over 57 years.

. . .our daughters, Donna and Karen, who both carry a piece of my
heart as part of their own.

. . .their daughters, Janelle, Karie and Emily, who in time may pass
along a bit of my heart to those who are destined to follow.

And a special note of thanks to my sounding board and friend, Robert
Thornberry, for not being afraid to point out what was--and was not--
good, and who came up with the comment that could well become the
book's theme: "When two hearts talk, love listens."

SECRETS YOU'LL WANT TO LEARN
ABOUT TWO HEARTS TALKING

This book is written in one of the most powerful formats used to express the language of love.

Its words move away from tradition, where the observer stands outside looking in, and instead draws one into active participation. One savors the honest, tender truths it offers, discovering the words he or she wants to say and longs to hear.

The power lies in the transmission, in the poetic format called Cinquain. Like Haiku, Cinquain is based on syllabic structure, but limited to five lines.

Line by line syllable count runs 2, 4, 6, 8, then goes back to 2 for the fifth line. Total syllable count is 22.

In typesetting, each line is set flush left, and contains only its allotted number of syllables. Thus each line is a different length. Part of Cinquain's charm is the inviting visual image it creates on paper.

The style was developed and perfected for the English language "as a form of short lyric that was both highly personal and tightly compressed in expression." The tight compression of words is what gives Two Hearts Talking its direction and power.

The technique is unforgiving in its stringent line and syllable requirements. Conversely, Cinquain is overpowering in the hands of one skilled at milking words, producing balanced conversations that speak smoothly, read and listen beautifully, easily drop into memory. They flow like wild honey on warm biscuits, and offer similar promise.

So relax. Read. Re-read. Think. Enjoy. Anticipate.
Love will begin to listen when your heart begins to talk.

TWO HEARTS TALKING

to my forever
Valentine who's
love taught
my heart
to love.

Lulnann

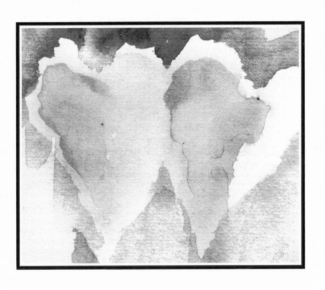

BEGINNING

Haunting . . .
mysterious . . .
how soul discovers soul
when magically two hearts begin
to talk.

JOURNEY

I walked
a lonely trail,
the same as you had done.
We met, and learned to fill our lives
with love.

DISCOVERY

We met . . .
and when our hearts
discovered matching souls
I knew that I had loved you all
my life.

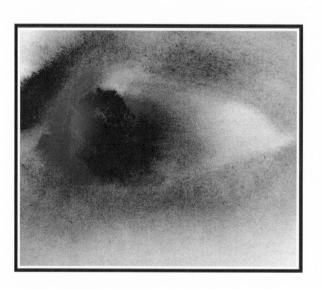

FIRE SONG

Your eyes . . .
glowing embers,
waiting to kindle flame . . .
I gazed at them, and fell in love
with you.

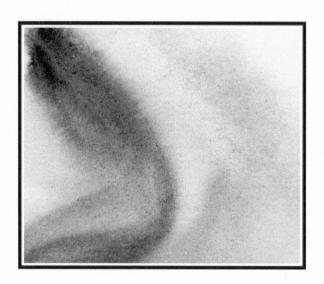

TOTAL IMAGE

You're there
in everything
I think and see and feel,
but that's because I'm so in love
with you.

MIND SONG

You live
beside the path
of all my special thoughts,
so every day I pass that way
. . . and smile.

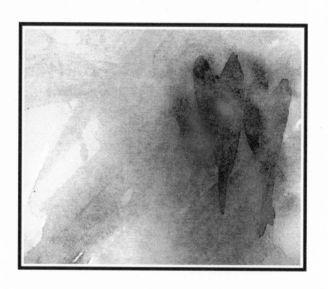

MY FRIEND

Somehow
I know I make
a difference in your life,
as you in mine . . . it's nice to be
so close.

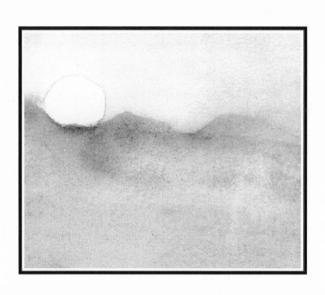

DAWN SONG

Morning.
I sing with joy
to celebrate the day.
You are the words and music of
my song.

DIRECTION

You may
have found your love
when eyes meet . . . and linger . . .
and slowly then he reaches for
your hand.

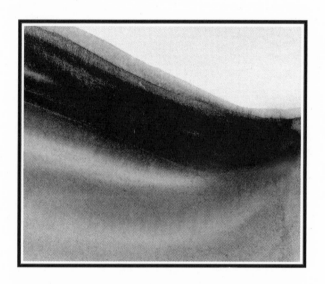

HAVEN

I'm safe
within your arms.
No harm can touch me here.
You are my friend, my light, my love,
my life.

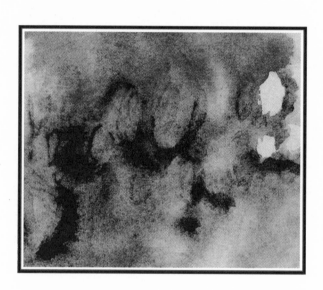

REASSURANCE

I *search*
across the crowd
and see your eyes respond . . .
Again we know our lives are wrapped
with love.

FOCUS

City,
bubbling life,
surging with excitement.
So much to see . . . but all I see
is you.

A MAGIC PLACE

Garden.
Rich with promise.
A place where color sings
and senses glow. It makes me think
of you.

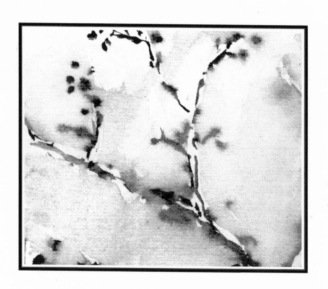

SPRING THOUGHT

Springtime . . .
season of hope,
awash with joy and love,
whose most important element
is you.

HARMONY

Darling,
you nestle here,
tucked in my loving arms,
and we find perfect balance in
our world.

VIEWPOINT

Mankind
sees its glories
in sunsets, pristine views
or distant stars. I simply look
at you.

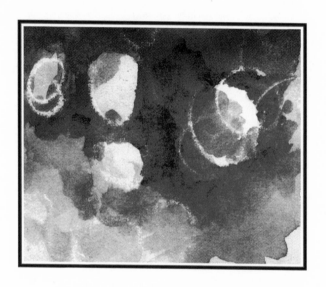

WELCOME

I *dream*
and you *appear*.
I *see*, and you *are there*.
You *live in every thought*, and I
rejoice.

HIDING PLACE

Island.
A *paradise*
beyond the realm of soul.
We sojourn there, and come away
refreshed.

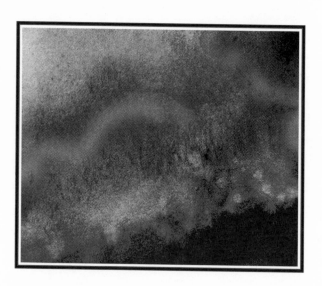

PROMISE

Softly
you wander through
the shadows of my mind,
assuring me I'll never be
alone.

STRENGTH

Night falls.
We're not afraid
when darkness stalks our world.
We're armored with the power of
our love.

MEANING

I feel
so much for you,
so much beyond my love,
beyond my dreams . . . You have become
my life.

NIGHT SONG

Day ends.
God lights the stars,
flowers scent the evening,
. . . but you are still the magic of
the night.

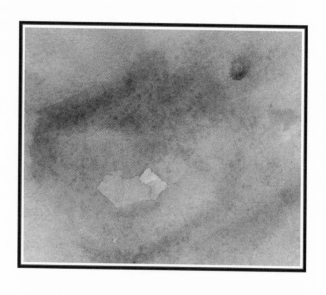

ALWAYS

I love
to hold your hand.
Quietly, it tells me
that you and I will never be
apart.

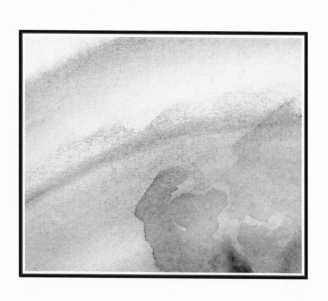

SECURE

The love
I feel for you
lives inside a rainbow
that always shines and never goes
away.

EVERYTHING

You are
soft breath of dawn,
a whisper in the night,
my song of love, the essence of
my life.

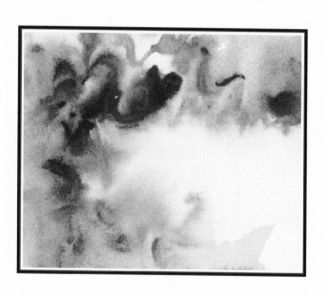

LINGUISTS

Lively
conversation . . .
The quiet touch of hands . . .
just two of many ways our hearts
can talk.

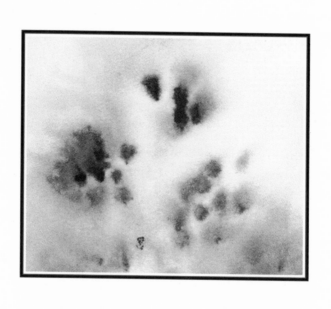

MAGNET

You call,
and I am there.
I beckon, you respond.
What powers this attraction is
our love.

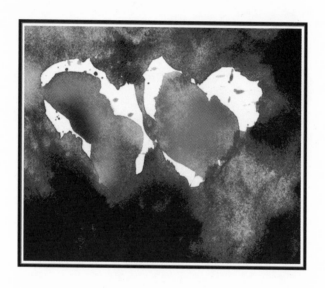

WHISPERS

I know
how near you are,
how deep and true your love.
I'm reassured by whispers in
the night.